THE ILLUSTRATED
ENCYCLOPEDIA

VOLUME 9

INDEX

Belitha Press

First published 1995 by
Macmillan Education Australia Pty Ltd

First published in the United Kingdom in 1995 by
Belitha Press Limited
31 Newington Green, London N16 9PU

Cataloguing in print data available from the British Library.

ISBN 1 85561 528 2 (Vol 9)
ISBN 1 85561 529 0 (Set)

Consultant: Frances Warhurst
UK editor: Maria O'Neill
Project editor: Jo Higgins

Typeset by Polar Design
Printed in Hong Kong

Acknowledgements

The author and publishers are grateful to the following for permission to reproduce copyright material:

Australian Antarctic Division, p. 10; Bill Bachman/ANT Photo Library, p. 39; Coo-ee Picture Library, pp. 17, 21, 24, 25, 35, 37, 47, 59; Bill Fagan, p. 22; General Motors Holden, p. 33; International Photographic Library, pp. 13, 53; NASA, pp. 42, 62; Northside Photographics, pp. 14, 20, 51, 60; Sporting-Pix, pp. 27, 40; Stock Photos, p.61; Silvestris/A.N.T. Photo Library, p. 29.

While every care has been taken to trace and acknowledge copyright, the publishers tender their apologies for any accidental infringement where copyright has proved untraceable.

CONTENTS

▼▼▼▼▼▼▼▼▼▼▼▼▼▼▼▼▼▼▼▼▼▼▼▼▼

How to use this encyclopedia   4

An information trail   6

Using the index   8

Index   10

Subject index   52

HOW TO USE THIS ENCYCLOPEDIA

The Illustrated Encyclopedia introduces you to the exciting world of knowledge. It has many features that will help you find what you are looking for. There are more than 300 entries arranged in alphabetical order. Each entry is one, two or four pages long.

The entries on a double-page spread begin with the letter which is highlighted on the alphabet strip.

The alphabet is printed across the top of each double-page spread.

The 'see also' box lists other topics that are connected to the one you are reading about.

Topic word

Each entry begins with an introduction which tells you the basic facts about the topic.

Labels explain different parts of an illustration.

Sub-headings introduce information about different aspects of the topic word.

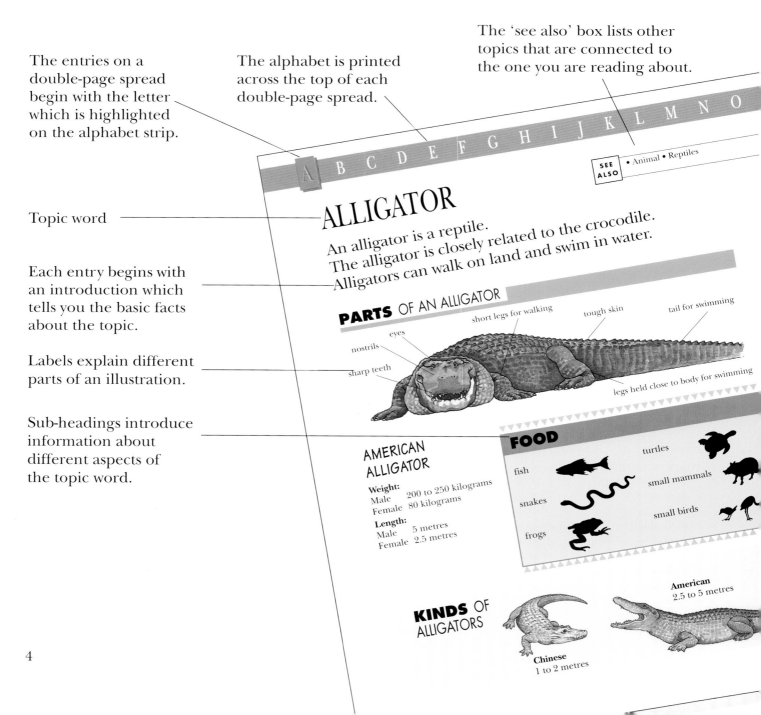

A B C D E F G H I J K L M N O

SEE ALSO • Animal • Reptiles

ALLIGATOR

An alligator is a reptile.
The alligator is closely related to the crocodile.
Alligators can walk on land and swim in water.

PARTS OF AN ALLIGATOR

nostrils
eyes
sharp teeth
short legs for walking
tough skin
tail for swimming
legs held close to body for swimming

AMERICAN ALLIGATOR

Weight:
Male   200 to 250 kilograms
Female 80 kilograms

Length:
Male   5 metres
Female 2.5 metres

FOOD

fish
snakes
frogs
turtles
small mammals
small birds

KINDS OF ALLIGATORS

Chinese
1 to 2 metres

American
2.5 to 5 metres

Guide words list the entries on a double-page spread. They are listed alphabetically.

The 'interesting fact' box tells you something interesting about the topic word.

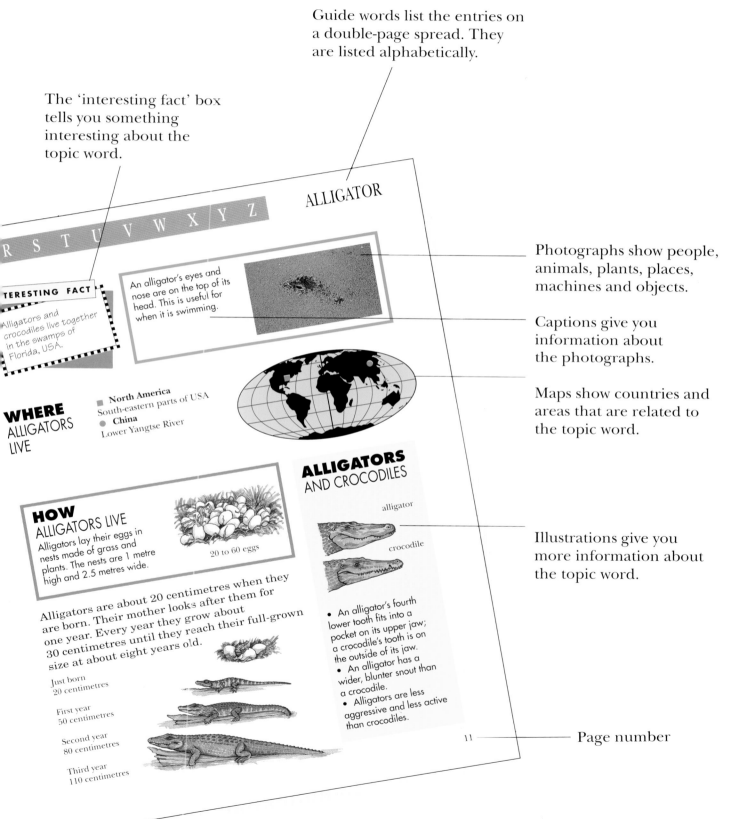

ALLIGATOR

R S T U V W X Y Z

TERESTING FACT

Alligators and crocodiles live together in the swamps of Florida, USA.

An alligator's eyes and nose are on the top of its head. This is useful for when it is swimming.

Photographs show people, animals, plants, places, machines and objects.

Captions give you information about the photographs.

WHERE
ALLIGATORS
LIVE

■ **North America**
South-eastern parts of USA
● **China**
Lower Yangtse River

Maps show countries and areas that are related to the topic word.

ALLIGATORS
AND CROCODILES

alligator

crocodile

HOW
ALLIGATORS LIVE
Alligators lay their eggs in nests made of grass and plants. The nests are 1 metre high and 2.5 metres wide.

20 to 60 eggs

Alligators are about 20 centimetres when they are born. Their mother looks after them for one year. Every year they grow about 30 centimetres until they reach their full-grown size at about eight years old.

Just born
20 centimetres

First year
50 centimetres

Second year
80 centimetres

Third year
110 centimetres

• An alligator's fourth lower tooth fits into a pocket on its upper jaw; a crocodile's tooth is on the outside of its jaw.
• An alligator has a wider, blunter snout than a crocodile.
• Alligators are less aggressive and less active than crocodiles.

Illustrations give you more information about the topic word.

11

Page number

5

AN INFORMATION TRAIL

The 'see also' box beside each topic word lists other topics that are related to the topic you are reading about. They can help you learn more about your topic.

- This tells you that alligators belong to the animal kingdom.
- It also tells you that alligators are reptiles.

Look up these topic words to find out about:
- the animal kingdom
- other animals that are reptiles.

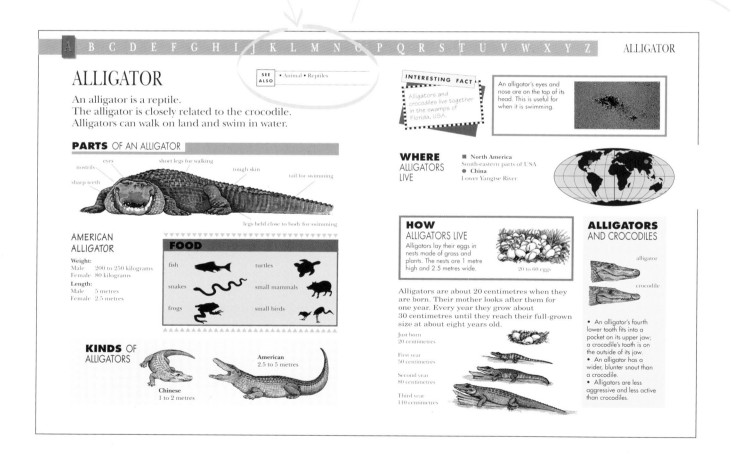

A B C D E F G H I J K L M N O P Q R S T U V W X Y Z   ALLIGATOR

ALLIGATOR

SEE ALSO • Animal • Reptiles

An alligator is a reptile.
The alligator is closely related to the crocodile.
Alligators can walk on land and swim in water.

PARTS OF AN ALLIGATOR

nostrils
eyes
short legs for walking
tough skin
sharp teeth
tail for swimming
legs held close to body for swimming

AMERICAN ALLIGATOR

Weight:
Male   200 to 250 kilograms
Female 80 kilograms
Length:
Male   5 metres
Female 2.5 metres

FOOD
fish   turtles
snakes   small mammals
frogs   small birds

KINDS OF ALLIGATORS

Chinese
1 to 2 metres

American
2.5 to 5 metres

INTERESTING FACT
Alligators and crocodiles live together in the swamps of Florida, USA.

An alligator's eyes and nose are on the top of its head. This is useful for when it is swimming.

WHERE ALLIGATORS LIVE
■ North America
South-eastern parts of USA
● China
Lower Yangtse River

HOW ALLIGATORS LIVE
Alligators lay their eggs in nests made of grass and plants. The nests are 1 metre high and 2.5 metres wide.

20 to 60 eggs

Alligators are about 20 centimetres when they are born. Their mother looks after them for one year. Every year they grow about 30 centimetres until they reach their full-grown size at about eight years old.

Just born
20 centimetres

First year
50 centimetres

Second year
80 centimetres

Third year
110 centimetres

ALLIGATORS AND CROCODILES

alligator

crocodile

- An alligator's fourth lower tooth fits into a pocket on its upper jaw; a crocodile's tooth is on the outside of its jaw.
- An alligator has a wider, blunter snout than a crocodile.
- Alligators are less aggressive and less active than crocodiles.

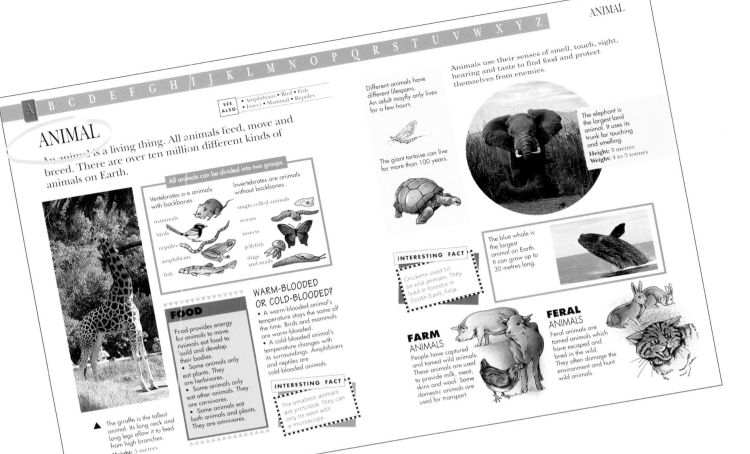

SEE ALSO • Amphibians • Bird • Fish • Insect • Mammal • Reptiles

ANIMAL

An animal is a living thing. All animals feed, move and breed. There are over ten million different kinds of animals on Earth.

All animals can be divided into two groups.

Vertebrates are animals with backbones.
mammals
birds
reptiles
amphibians
fish

Invertebrates are animals without backbones.
single-celled animals
worms
insects
jellyfish
slugs and snails

FOOD

Food provides energy for animals to move. Animals eat food to build and develop their bodies.
• Some animals only eat plants. They are herbivores.
• Some animals only eat other animals. They are carnivores.
• Some animals eat both animals and plants. They are omnivores.

WARM-BLOODED OR COLD-BLOODED?

• A warm-blooded animal's temperature stays the same all the time. Birds and mammals are warm-blooded.
• A cold-blooded animal's temperature changes with its surroundings. Amphibians and reptiles are cold-blooded animals.

INTERESTING FACT
The smallest animals are protozoa. They can only be seen with a microscope.

▲ The giraffe is the tallest animal. Its long neck and long legs allow it to feed from high branches.
Height: 5 metres

Different animals have different lifespans. An adult mayfly only lives for a few hours.

The giant tortoise can live for more than 100 years.

Animals use their senses of smell, touch, sight, hearing and taste to find food and protect themselves from enemies.

The elephant is the largest land animal. It uses its trunk for touching and smelling.
Height: 3 metres
Weight: 4 to 5 tonnes

The blue whale is the largest animal on Earth. It can grow up to 30 metres long.

INTERESTING FACT
Chickens used to be wild animals. They lived in forests in South East Asia.

FARM ANIMALS

People have captured and tamed wild animals. These animals are used to provide milk, meat, skins and wool. Some domestic animals are used for transport.

FERAL ANIMALS

Feral animals are tamed animals which have escaped and bred in the wild. They often damage the environment and hunt wild animals.

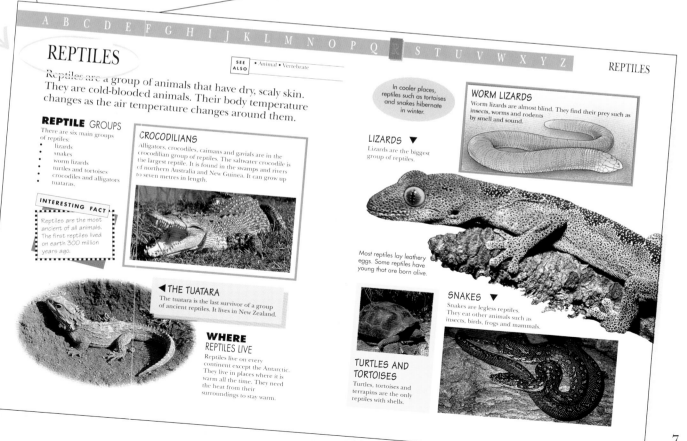

REPTILES

SEE ALSO • Animal • Vertebrate

Reptiles are a group of animals that have dry, scaly skin. They are cold-blooded animals. Their body temperature changes as the air temperature changes around them.

REPTILE GROUPS

There are six main groups of reptiles:
• lizards
• snakes
• worm lizards
• turtles and tortoises
• crocodiles and alligators
• tuataras.

INTERESTING FACT
Reptiles are the most ancient of all animals. The first reptiles lived on earth 300 million years ago.

CROCODILIANS

Alligators, crocodiles, caimans and gavials are in the crocodilian group of reptiles. The saltwater crocodile is the largest reptile. It is found in the swamps and rivers of northern Australia and New Guinea. It can grow up to seven metres in length.

◄ THE TUATARA
The tuatara is the last survivor of a group of ancient reptiles. It lives in New Zealand.

WHERE REPTILES LIVE

Reptiles live on every continent except the Antarctic. They live in places where it is warm all the time. They need the heat from their surroundings to stay warm.

In cooler places, reptiles such as tortoises and snakes hibernate in winter.

WORM LIZARDS

Worm lizards are almost blind. They find their prey such as insects, worms and rodents by smell and sound.

LIZARDS ▼
Lizards are the biggest group of reptiles.

Most reptiles lay leathery eggs. Some reptiles have young that are born alive.

SNAKES ▼
Snakes are legless reptiles. They eat other animals such as insects, birds, frogs and mammals.

TURTLES AND TORTOISES

Turtles, tortoises and terrapins are the only reptiles with shells.

USING THE INDEX

▼▼▼▼▼▼▼▼▼▼▼▼▼▼▼▼▼▼▼▼▼▼

The index lists all the subjects in the encyclopedia. You can find any subject by using the index which is arranged in alphabetical order.

Where can I find out about alligators?

- Look up your topic to find out which volume to look in.

airport
    Volume 1   4–5, **8–9**
air traffic control
    see **airport**
alligator
    Volume 1   **10–11**
    Volume 7   20–21
allosaurus
    see **dinosaur**
alphabet
    Volume 1   **12**
aluminium
    Volume 1   **13**
    Volume 5   45–46
    Volume 7   18
ambulance
    Volume 1   **14**
    Volume 2   54–55

- The page numbers are listed after each volume. They tell you which page to look on.

- Page numbers in bold type tell you that the topic has its own entry.

When you cannot find the topic you are looking for in alphabetical order in the encyclopedia, then use the index. It will tell you which volume to look in and which page to turn to.

Where can I find out about crocodiles?

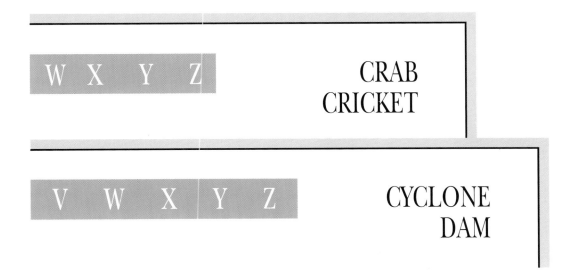

W X Y Z

CRAB
CRICKET

V W X Y Z

CYCLONE
DAM

The subject 'crocodile' is missing in its alphabetical order in Volume 2. Look up 'crocodile' in the index.

A 'see' reference tells you that the information you are looking for is under other headings. Look up 'Alligator' and 'Reptiles' to find information about crocodiles.

crayfish
    see **pond life**
credit card
    see **money**
cricket
    Volume 2 **41**
crocodile
    see **alligator**
    see **reptiles**
crops
    see **farming**

Aa

INDEX

Page numbers printed in bold mean that there is an entry for that subject in the encyclopedia. Some subjects are followed by a 'see' reference. This means that your subject can be found under the entry listed.

Antarctica

aeroplane
    Volume 1 **4–5,** 8–9
    Volume 2 31
    Volume 4 60
    Volume 8 19
Africa
    see **continent**
air
    Volume 1 **6–7,** 30
    Volume 6 52
    Volume 8 47
airport
    Volume 1 4–5, **8–9**
air traffic control
    see **airport**
alligator
    Volume 1 **10–11**
    Volume 7 20–21
allosaurus
    see **dinosaur**
alphabet
    Volume 1 **12**
aluminium
    Volume 1 **13**
    Volume 5 45–46
    Volume 7 18
ambulance
    Volume 1 **14**
    Volume 2 54–55
amphibian
    Volume 1 **15**
    Volume 3 58–59
    Volume 8 30

animal
    Volume 1 15, **16–17**, 48–51
    Volume 2 10, 36–37, 49
    Volume 3 10–11, 15, 30–31
    Volume 4 58–59, 61
    Volume 5 6–7, 26–27, 40, 51
    Volume 6 5, 8, 11
    Volume 7 20–21, 30–31
    Volume 8 4, 26, 30, 56–57
ant
    Volume 1 **18**
Antarctica
    Volume 1 **19**
    Volume 2 35
    Volume 4 58–59
antelope
    see **ungulates**
antlers
    see **deer**
ape
    Volume 1 **20–21**
    Volume 5 40, 54–55
arachnid
    see **spider**
archery
    Volume 1 **22**
    Volume 2 15
Arctic
    Volume 1 **23**
Asia
    see **continent**
astronaut
    Volume 1 **24–25**
    Volume 5 58–59
    Volume 7 58, 59
astronomy
    Volume 1 **26–27**
    Volume 7 62
    Volume 8 8–9
athletics
    Volume 1 **28–29**
    Volume 6 20–21
atlas
    see **book**

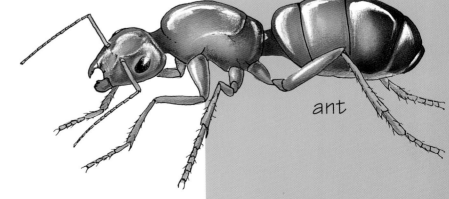

ant

balloon

atmosphere
    Volume 1 6–7, **30**
Australia
    see **continent**
autumn
    see **season**
avalanche
    Volume 1 **31**
axolotl
    see **pet**

baleen whales
    see **whale**
ball bearings
    see **wheel**
ballet
    Volume 1 **32–33**
    Volume 2 44
    Volume 6 23
balloon
    Volume 1 **34–35**
    Volume 8 53
bamboo
    see **grass**
bank
    Volume 1 **36**
    Volume 2 31
barcode
    see **shop**
barley
    see **bread**
    see **grass**
baseball
    Volume 1 **37**
basketball
    Volume 1 **38**
bat
    Volume 1 **39**
battery
    see **electricity**
    see **torch**
bauxite
    see **aluminium**

Bb

bear
 Volume 1 **40–41**
 Volume 5 40
 Volume 6 30–31
beaver
 see **dam**
 see **rodent**
bee
 Volume 1 **42–43**
 Volume 3 40–43
 Volume 4 59
beef cattle
 see **cattle**
beetle
 Volume 1 **44**
 Volume 4 58–59
 Volume 5 18
bell
 Volume 1 **45**
berry
 see **fruit**
bicycle
 Volume 1 **46–47**
 Volume 5 62
 Volume 8 18
binoculars
 see **telescope**
bird
 Volume 1 **48–51**
 Volume 2 12, 64
 Volume 3 15
 Volume 5 14
 Volume 6 8, 24, 25, 34–35, 36–37,
      40–41, 54–55, 62
 Volume 7 40–41
 Volume 8 30, 34–35
bison
 Volume 8 26
blood
 Volume 1 **52**
 Volume 4 37, 55
 Volume 5 36
boa
 see **snake**

bat

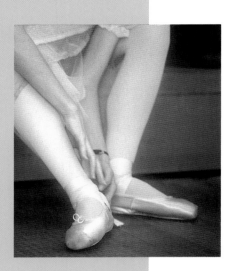

ballet

boat
 Volume 1 **53**
 Volume 2 13
 Volume 4 52, 54
 Volume 7 34, 46–47, 63
 Volume 8 60
bones
 see **human body**
 see **skeleton**
 see **X–ray**
book
 Volume 1 **54–55**
 Volume 5 24–25
 Volume 6 58–59
botanic gardens
 see **garden**
brachiosaurus
 see **dinosaur**
Braille
 see **school**
brain
 Volume 1 **56–57**
 Volume 3 4, 23
 Volume 4 55
 Volume 6 11
 Volume 7 51
 Volume 8 4
bread
 Volume 1 **58**
 Volume 3 24–25, 44–45
breathing
 see **lung**
 see **nose**
brick
 Volume 1 **59**
 Volume 4 52–53
bridge
 Volume 1 **60–61**
 Volume 7 26
 Volume 8 18–19
brittle star
 see **echinoderm**
brontosaurus
 see **dinosaur**

bronze
  see **metal**
budgerigar
  see **parrot**
bus
  see **transport**
butterflies and moths
  Volume 1 16, **62–64**
  Volume 4 58–59

calendar
  Volume 2 **4–5**
  Volume 5 56–57
camel
  Volume 2 **6–7,** 49
  Volume 5 56–57
camera
  Volume 2 **8–9**
  Volume 4 16
  Volume 8 10–11
camouflage
  Volume 1 49
  Volume 2 **10**
  Volume 3 31
  Volume 4 12, 35
  Volume 5 4
  Volume 6 62
  Volume 8 43
camping
  Volume 2 **11**
canary
  Volume 1 48–51
  Volume 2 **12**
  Volume 6 38–39
canoe
  Volume 2 **13**
  Volume 8 18–19
car
  see **motor car**
  see **transport**
  see **wheel**
carbohydrates
  see **food**
  see **fish**

Cc

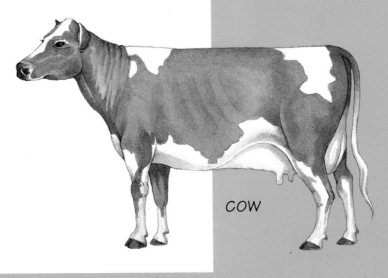

COW

15

Cc

carbon dioxide
    see **blood**
    see **gas**
    see **leaf**
    see **plant**
    see **tree**
carnival
    see **festival**
carnivore
    see **animal**
cartoon
    Volume 2 **14**
castle
    Volume 2 **15**
cat
    Volume 2 **16–17**
    Volume 5 4–5, 32–33
    Volume 6 38–39
caterpillar
    see **butterflies and moths**
    see **insect**
cattle
    Volume 2 **18–19**
    Volume 3 25
    Volume 4 28
    Volume 8 26, 61
cave
    Volume 1 55
    Volume 2 **20–21**
    Volume 4 52
chameleon
    see **camouflage**
chess
    see **games**
chicken
    see **animal**
    see **farming**
    see **pet**
chimpanzee
    see **ape**
chipmunk
    see **rodents**
chrysalis
    see **butterflies and moths**

camel

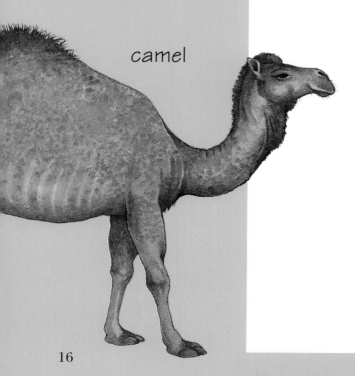

circulatory system
    see **blood**
    see **human body**
circus
    Volume 2 **22–23**
clock
    Volume 2 **24**
    Volume 6 64
clothes
    Volume 2 **25**
cloud
    Volume 2 **26**
    Volume 7 10–11
    Volume 8 44–47
coal
    Volume 2 **27**, 32
    Volume 3 26, 62–63
    Volume 5 50
cold-blooded animals
    see **animal**
    see **frog**
    see **lizard**
    see **reptiles**
    see **snake**
colour
    Volume 2 **28**
    Volume 5 29
    Volume 6 59
    Volume 7 12–13
comet
    see **astronomy**
compost
    Volume 2 **29**
    Volume 3 49
    Volume 7 18
computer
    Volume 2 **30–31**
    Volume 6 58–59
    Volume 7 27
    Volume 8 17
condor
    see **vulture**
cone shell
    see **snail**

castle

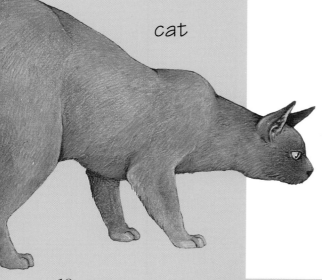

cat

conservation
    Volume 2 **32–33**
    Volume 3 33
    Volume 5 5
    Volume 7 14
    Volume 8 64
constellation
    see **star**
continent
    Volume 2 **34–35**
copper
    see **metal**
coral
    Volume 1 16–17
    Volume 2 **36–37**
    Volume 4 64
corn
    see **bread**
    see **grass**
cotton
    Volume 2 25, **38–39**
    Volume 3 25
crab
    Volume 1 16–17
    Volume 2 **40**
    Volume 7 40–41
crayfish
    see **pond life**
credit card
    see **money**
cricket
    Volume 2 **41**
crocodile
    see **alligator**
    see **reptiles**
crops
    see **farming**
cuttlefish
    see **octopus**
cyclone
    Volume 2 **42**
    Volume 8 44–47, 52–53

dam
    Volume 2 **43**
    Volume 4 63
    Volume 8 37
dancing
    Volume 1 32–33
    Volume 2 **44**
days of the week
    Volume 2 4–5, **45–46**
    Volume 5 56–57
deciduous trees
    see **tree**
decimal system
    see **number**
deer
    Volume 2 **46–47**
    Volume 8 26
dentist
    see **doctor**
    see **X–ray**
desert
    Volume 2 **48–49**
    Volume 3 6
detective
    see **police**
dew
    see **weather**
diamond
    see **gem**
digestion
    Volume 2 **50–51**
    Volume 3 44–45
    Volume 4 55
dinosaur
    Volume 2 **52–53**
    Volume 3 53
diplodocus
    see **dinosaur**
doctor
    Volume 2 **54–55**
    Volume 4 50–51
    Volume 8 58

duck

Dd

dancing

dodo
see **bird**
see **endangered species**
dog
Volume 2 **56–57**
Volume 6 51
doll
Volume 2 **58**
dolphin
Volume 2 **59**
Volume 3 5
Volume 5 40
dragon
Volume 2 **60**
dragonfly
Volume 2 **61**
Volume 6 54–55
drama
Volume 2 **62**
Volume 6 60–61
drug
Volume 2 54–55, **63**
duck
Volume 1 48–51
Volume 2 **64**

ears
Volume 3 **4–5**
Volume 7 57
Earth
Volume 1 30
Volume 2 4, 45
Volume 3 **6–7**, 12
Volume 4 30
Volume 5 58–59
Volume 6 14–15, 44–45
Volume 8 28
earthquake
Volume 3 **8**
earthworm
Volume 2 29
Volume 3 **9**
Volume 4 61
Volume 8 56–57

echinoderm
Volume 3 **10–11**
echolocation
see **ears**
eclipse
Volume 3 **12**
ecology
Volume 3 **13**
ecosystem
see **ecology**
see **forest**
see **grassland**
see **lake**
see **pond life**
see **rain forest**
see **river**
see **seashore life**
eel
Volume 3 **14**
egg
Volume 1 48
Volume 2 52
Volume 3 **15**
electricity
Volume 3 **16–17**, 62–63
Volume 5 28
elephant
Volume 1 17
Volume 3 5, **18–19**
endangered animals
see **elephant**
see **endangered species**
see **koala**
see **national park**
see **panda**
see **rhinoceros**
see **whale**
see **wolf**
see **zoo**
endangered species
Volume 3 19, **20**
Volume 5 17
Volume 6 30

eggs

Ee

firefighters

Volume 7 22–23
Volume 8 49, 55
energy
  see **conservation**
  see **electricity**
  see **fuel**
  see **heat**
  see **machine**
  see **Sun**
  see **weather**
equator
  Volume 3 **21**
  Volume 7 43
Europe
  see **continent**
evergreen trees
  see **leaf**
exercise
  Volume 3 **22**
  Volume 4 32–33, 37
eye
  Volume 3 **23**
  Volume 4 55

farming
  Volume 2 47
  Volume 3 **24–25,** 43
  Volume 4 24–25, 28
  Volume 6 27, 62
fax machine
  see **telephone**
feral animal
  see **animal**
fern
  Volume 3 **26**
  Volume 6 46–47
festival
  Volume 3 **27**
  Volume 2 58, 60
film
  see **camera**
firefighters
  Volume 3 **28–29**

fish
    Volume 1 16–17
    Volume 3 14, **30–31**, 32–33
    Volume 4 22–23
    Volume 6 54–55
    Volume 7 37, 44–45
    Volume 8 30
fishing
    Volume 3 **32–33**
flag
    Volume 3 **34–35**
flea
    Volume 3 **36**
flies
    Volume 3 **37**
floating
    Volume 3 **38**
    Volume 7 47
flood
    Volume 3 **39**
flower
    Volume 3 **40–43**, 60–61
    Volume 6 46–47
    Volume 8 29
fog
    see **weather**
food
    Volume 1 58
    Volume 3 24–25, 32–33, **44–45**
    Volume 6 13
    Volume 7 19
    Volume 8 29, 32
food chain
    Volume 2 33
    Volume 3 13, **46**
    Volume 6 53
football
    Volume 3 **47**
    Volume 7 32–33, 56
forest
    Volume 3 7, **48–51**
    Volume 7 14–15
    Volume 8 20–21

fish

frog

fossil
    Volume 2 52
    Volume 3 **52–53**
fossil fuel
    see **coal**
    see **fuel**
    see **gas**
    see **oil**
fox
    Volume 3 **54–55**
fraction
    Volume 3 **56**
    Volume 6 12
friction
    Volume 3 **57**
frill-necked lizard
    see **lizard**
frog
    Volume 1 15
    Volume 3 **58–59**
    Volume 5 27
    Volume 6 54–55
frost
    see **weather**
fruit
    Volume 3 25, 41, **60–61**
    Volume 6 46–47
fuel
    Volume 2 27
    Volume 3 **62–63**
    Volume 4 8–9
    Volume 6 18–19
fungi
    Volume 3 48–49, **64**

galaxy
    Volume 1 26
    Volume 4 **4**
    Volume 8 28
games
    Volume 4 **5**
garden
    Volume 3 40–43
    Volume 4 **6–7**

Volume 6 46–47
Volume 8 20–21

gas
Volume 1 6–7, 30, 34
Volume 4 **8–9**

gears
see **wheel**

gem
Volume 4 **10–11**

gibbon
see **ape**

giraffe
Volume 1 16
Volume 4 **12–13**
Volume 8 26

glacier
Volume 4 **14–15,** 56

glass
Volume 4 **16**
Volume 7 18

glider
Volume 4 **17**, 36

goat
Volume 3 25
Volume 4 **18–19**
Volume 5 40
Volume 6 39

gold
Volume 4 10, **20–21**
Volume 5 46–47

goldfish
Volume 4 **22–23**
Volume 6 39

gorilla
see **ape**

grain
see **bread**

granite
see **minerals**

grass
Volume 3 25, 40–42
Volume 4 **24–25,** 28–29
Volume 6 46–47

Gg

gymnastics

Gg

grasshopper
    Volume 4 **26–27**, 58–59
grassland
    Volume 3 25
    Volume 4 24–25, **28–29**
gravity
    Volume 1 24–25
    Volume 4 **30**
    Volume 5 59
greenhouse effect
    see **fuel**
guinea pig
    Volume 4 **31**
    Volume 6 39
gun powder
    see **invention**
gymnastics
    Volume 3 22
    Volume 4 **32–33**

habitat
    see **conservation**
    see **grass**
    see **grassland**
    see **pond life**
    see **rain forest**
    see **seashore life**
hail
    see **weather**
hair
    Volume 4 **34–35**
    Volume 7 51
hamster
    see **pet**
hang-gliding
    Volume 4 17, **36**
hare
    see **rabbit**
hay
    see **grass**
heart
    Volume 3 22
    Volume 4 **37,** 55

giraffe

heat
    Volume 4 **38**
hedgehog
    Volume 4 35, **39**
helicopter
    Volume 1 14
    Volume 4 **40**
    Volume 8 18–19
herbivore
    see **animal**
    see **ungulates**
heritage
    Volume 4 **41**
hibernate
    see **hedgehog**
    see **season**
hippopotamus
    Volume 4 **42–43**
    Volume 8 26
hobby
    Volume 4 **44**
    Volume 6 56
hockey
    Volume 4 **45**
hologram
    see **laser**
horse
    Volume 4 **46–47,** 48–49
    Volume 5 40
    Volume 8 26
horse riding
    Volume 4 46–47, **48–49**
hospital
    Volume 1 14
    Volume 2 31, 54–55
    Volume 4 **50–51**
hot-air balloons
    see **balloon**
house
    Volume 2 20
    Volume 4 **52–53**
hovercraft
    Volume 4 **54**
    Volume 8 18–19

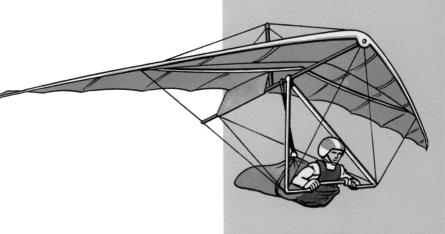

hang-gliding

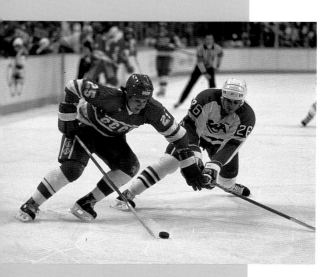

ice hockey

human body
    Volume 1   52, 56–57
    Volume 2   50–51
    Volume 3   4–5, 23
    Volume 4   34–35, 37, **55**
    Volume 5   26–27, 36
    Volume 6   11
    Volume 7   49, 51
    Volume 8   4, 5
hurricane
    see **cyclone**
hydro-electric power station
    see **electricity**

ice
    see **avalanche**
    see **glacier**
    see **iceberg**
    see **water**
    see **weather**
iceberg
    Volume 4   15, **56**
ice hockey
    see **hockey**
ice skating
    Volume 4   **57**
insect
    Volume 1   16, 18, 42–43, 44, 62–64
    Volume 2   10, 61
    Volume 3   36, 37, 40–41, 53
    Volume 4   26, 27, **58–59**, 61
    Volume 5   18, 27
    Volume 6   8, 54–55
internal combustion engine
    see **motor car**
intestine
    see **digestion**
invention
    Volume 4   **60**
    Volume 7   8–9, 63
    Volume 8   7, 8, 11, 58
invertebrate
    Volume 1   16
    Volume 4   **61**

iron and steel
    Volume 4 **62**
    Volume 5 30, 46–47, 50
irrigation
    Volume 4 **63**
island
    Volume 4 **64**

jaguars and leopards
    Volume 2 16–17
    Volume 5 **4–5**
jellyfish
    Volume 4 61
    Volume 5 **6–7**
jerboa
    see **rodents**
jet engine
    Volume 5 **8–9**
Jupiter
    see **planet**

kangaroo
    Volume 5 **10–11,** 40, 44
kayaking
    see **canoe**
kite
    Volume 5 **12–13**
kiwi
    Volume 5 **14**
knight
    Volume 5 **15**
knot
    Volume 5 **16**
koala
    Volume 5 **17**, 40

ladybird
    Volume 4 59
    Volume 5 **18**
lake
    Volume 3 39
    Volume 5 **19**
lammergeyer
    see **vulture**

jaguar

Ll

laser
> Volume 5 **20,** 28–29

latitude and longitude
> Volume 5 **21,** 42–43

leaf
> Volume 3 40–43, 46, 48–51
> Volume 4 6–7, 24–25
> Volume 5 **22–23**
> Volume 6 46–47
> Volume 8 20–21

leap year
> *see* **calendar**

lens
> *see* **camera**
> *see* **glass**

leopard
> *see* **jaguars and leopards**

library
> Volume 1 54–55
> Volume 5 **24–25**

life cycle
> Volume 5 **26–27**

light
> Volume 3 16–17, 23
> Volume 5 20, **28–29**
> Volume 7 12–13, 64
> Volume 8 14

lighthouse
> Volume 5 **30–31**

lion
> Volume 4 28–29
> Volume 5 **32–33**

lizard
> Volume 2 16–17
> Volume 5 **34–35**
> Volume 7 20–21

llamas
> *see* **ungulates**

locust
> *see* **grasshopper**

lorry
> *see* **transport**
> *see* **truck**

lizard

lung
    Volume 1 52
    Volume 4 37, 55
    Volume 5 **36**
    Volume 6 11

machine
    Volume 2 30–31
    Volume 5 **37**
    Volume 7 27
    Volume 8 50–51
magic
    Volume 5 **38**
magnet
    Volume 5 **39**
mammal
    Volume 1 16, 20–21, 39, 40–41
    Volume 2 6–7, 16–17, 18–19, 46–47,
               56–57, 59
    Volume 3 15, 18–19, 54–55
    Volume 4 12–13, 18–19, 31, 34–35, 39,
               42–43, 46–47
    Volume 5 4–5, 26, 32–33, **40**, 44, 54–55
    Volume 6 8, 30–31
    Volume 7 4–5, 16–17, 22–23, 30–31,
               38–39
    Volume 8 26, 30, 42–43, 48–49, 54–55,
               61, 62–63
mammoth
    Volume 5 **41**
mangroves
    see **rain forest**
map
    Volume 5 **42–43**
    Volume 7 26
marble
    see **quarry**
    see **rocks**
Mars
    see **planet**
    see **Sun**
marsupial
    Volume 5 10–11, 17, 40, **44**

mining

Mm

measurement
Volume 5 **45**
medicine
see **doctor**
see **drug**
Mercury
see **planet**
see **Sun**
mercury
see **metal**
metal
Volume 1 13
Volume 4 20–21, 62
Volume 5 **46–47**
meteor
Volume 5 **48**
mice
see **pet**
see **rat**
migration
see **bird**
Milky Way
see **galaxy**
see **Universe**
millet
see **grass**
minerals
Volume 5 **49**
Volume 6 64
mining
Volume 1 13
Volume 2 27
Volume 4 9, 20–21, 62
Volume 5 47, **50**
Volume 6 18–19
mist
see **weather**
molluscs
Volume 5 **51**
Volume 7 52–53
money
Volume 1 36
Volume 5 **52–53**

monkey

Mm

monkey
  Volume 5 **54–55**
monotreme
  see **egg**
  see **mammal**
months of the year
  Volume 2 4–5, 45
  Volume 5 **56–57**
Moon
  Volume 1 24–25
  Volume 2 4
  Volume 3 12
  Volume 4 30
  Volume 5 **58–59**
  Volume 7 35
moose
  see **deer**
moth
  see **butterflies and moths**
motor car
  Volume 5 **60–61**
  Volume 7 26
  Volume 8 18–19
motorcycle
  Volume 5 **62**
  Volume 8 18–19
motorway
  see **road**
mountain
  Volume 3 6
  Volume 5 **63**
mouth
  see **digestion**
  see **human body**
mushroom
  see **fungi**
music
  Volume 1 32–33, 45
  Volume 2 23, 44
  Volume 5 **64**
  Volume 6 22–23
  Volume 8 59

machines

nuts

name
  Volume 6 **4–5**
national park
  Volume 3 20
  Volume 6 **6–7**
natural gas
  see **fuel**
  see **gas**
Neptune
  see **planet**
  see **Sun**
nerves
  see **brain**
nervous system
  see **human body**
nest
  Volume 1 48
  Volume 2 12, 64
  Volume 5 14
  Volume 6 **8**, 24, 25, 34–35,
  40–41, 62
netball
  Volume 6 **9**
newspaper
  Volume 6 **10,** 32–33, 58–59
newt
  see **amphibian**
nomad
  see **desert**
  see **grassland**
North America
  see **continent**
North Pole
  see **Arctic**
  see **Earth**
  see **latitude and longitude**
Northern Hemisphere
  see **equator**
nose
  Volume 4 55
  Volume 5 36
  Volume 6 **11**
number
  Volume 6 **12**

Oo

nut
> Volume 3 60–61
> Volume 6 **13,** 46–47

oasis
> *see* **desert**

oats
> *see* **bread**
> *see* **grass**

observatory
> *see* **astronomy**
> *see* **telescope**

ocean
> Volume 3 7
> Volume 6 **14–15**
> Volume 8 36–37

octopus
> Volume 6 **16–17**

oesophagus
> *see* **digestion**

oil
> Volume 2 32
> Volume 3 38, 57, 62
> Volume 6 **18–19**, 48

Olympic Games
> Volume 4 33, 57
> Volume 6 **20–21**
> Volume 7 50
> Volume 8 40–41

omnivore
> *see* **animal**

opossum
> *see* **marsupial**

optical fibres
> *see* **telephone**

orchard
> *see* **fruit**

orchestra
> Volume 1 32
> Volume 5 64
> Volume 6 **22–23**
> Volume 8 59

ordinal number
> *see* **number**

owl

Oo

organic farm
see **farming**
ostrich
Volume 6 **24**
owl
Volume 6 **25**
oxygen
see **air**
see **atmosphere**
see **blood**
see **exercise**
see **fish**
see **gas**
see **plant**
see **tree**
oyster
Volume 6 **26–27**
ozone layer
see **atmosphere**

painting
Volume 6 **28–29**
palaeontologist
see **fossil**
panda
Volume 1 40–41
Volume 3 20
Volume 6 **30–31**
panther
see **jaguars and leopards**
paper
Volume 1 54–55
Volume 6 10, **32–33**
Volume 7 18
Volume 8 21
papyrus
see **paper**
parasite
see **flea**
see **rhinoceros**
see **worm**
parrot
Volume 6 **34–35**

ostrich

pearl
see **oyster**
penguin
Volume 6 **36–37**
penicillin
see **drug**
pet
Volume 2 12, 16–17, 56–57
Volume 4 22–23, 31, 46–47, 48–49
Volume 6 **38–39**
Volume 7 4–5
petroleum
see **oil**
photograph
see **camera**
photosynthesis
see **leaf**
see **plant**
pig
see **farming**
see **ungulates**
pigeon
Volume 6 **40–41**
pirate
Volume 6 **42–43**
planet
Volume 1 26–27
Volume 6 **44–45**
Volume 7 35
Volume 8 28
plankton
see **ocean**
plant
Volume 1 23
Volume 2 49
Volume 3 26, 40–43, 48–51, 60–61
Volume 4 6–7, 22–23
Volume 5 22–23, 27
Volume 6 **46–47**
Volume 7 13
Volume 8 20–21
plastic
Volume 6 **48**
Volume 7 18

puppet

Pp

penguin

platypus
    Volume 5 40
    Volume 6 **49**
Pluto
    see **planet**
    see **Sun**
polar bear
    see **bear**
    see **camouflage**
police
    Volume 6 **50–51**
    Volume 7 7
pollen
    see **bee**
    see **flower**
pollution
    Volume 2 32
    Volume 3 20, 63
    Volume 5 61
    Volume 6 19, **52–53**
    Volume 8 19
pond life
    Volume 3 13, 30–31, 58–59
    Volume 4 58–59
    Volume 6 **54–55**
postal service
    Volume 4 44
    Volume 6 **56–57**
    Volume 8 19
printing
    Volume 1 54–55
    Volume 6 10, 32–33, **58–59**
protein
    see **food**
protozoa
    see **animal**
    see **invertebrate**
puffin
    see **bird**
    see **seashore life**
pulley
    see **wheel**
puppet
    Volume 6 **60–61**

python
   see **snake**

quail
   Volume 6 **62**
quarry
   Volume 6 **63,** 64
quartz
   Volume 5 49
   Volume 6 **64**
quill
   see **hair**

rabbit
   Volume 1 17
   Volume 3 5
   Volume 7 **4–5**
radar
   Volume 7 **6–7**
radio
   Volume 4 60
   Volume 7 **8–9**
   Volume 8 8
radio telescope
   see **telescope**
raft
   see **transport**
rain
   Volume 7 **10–11,** 12–13
   Volume 8 36, 44–47
rainbow
   Volume 5 29
   Volume 7 **12–13**
rain forest
   Volume 3 48–49
   Volume 7 **14–15**
rat
   Volume 7 **16–17**, 30
recycling
   Volume 1 13
   Volume 2 29
   Volume 4 16
   Volume 5 47
   Volume 6 33, 48
   Volume 7 **18**

recycling

Rr

river

reflection
    see **light**
refraction
    see **light**
refrigerator
    Volume 7 **19**
reindeer
    see **deer**
reptiles
    Volume 1 10–11, 16–17
    Volume 3 15
    Volume 5 34–35
    Volume 7 **20–21,** 54–55
    Volume 8 24–25, 30
reservoir
    see **dam**
    see **water**
respiratory system
    see **human body**
rhinoceros
    Volume 7 **22–23**
rice
    see **bread**
    see **farming**
    see **grass**
river
    Volume 3 39
    Volume 4 14–15
    Volume 7 10, **24–25**
    Volume 8 36–37
road
    Volume 7 **26**
    Volume 8 18–19
robot
    Volume 7 **27**
rock painting
    see **cave**
rock pool
    see **seashore life**
rocks
    Volume 1 13, 31
    Volume 2 27
    Volume 3 6–7
    Volume 4 10–11, 62
    Volume 5 46–47, 49, 58

Ss

Volume 6 63
Volume 7 **28–29**
rodents
Volume 4 31
Volume 7 16–17, **30–31**
Rugby
Volume 3 47
Volume 7 **32–33**

sailing
Volume 1 53
Volume 7 **34**
Volume 8 40, 60
salamander
see **amphibian**
salmon
see **life cycle**
satellite
Volume 1 27
Volume 2 42
Volume 5 43
Volume 7 **35**, 58, 59
Volume 8 7, 11, 47
Saturn
see **planet**
see **Sun**
school
Volume 7 9, **36**
sea
see **flood**
see **ocean**
seahorse
Volume 7 **37**
seal
Volume 7 **38–39**
seashore life
Volume 1 44–47
Volume 2 40
Volume 3 10–11, 13, 30–31
Volume 4 61
Volume 5 6–7, 51
Volume 6 16–17, 26–27
Volume 7 38–39, **40–41**, 52–53
Volume 8 56–57

rhinoceros

satellite

season
Volume 7 **42–43**
seaweed
see **plant**
see **seashore life**
sedimentary rock
see **fossil**
see **rocks**
seed
see **flower**
see **fruit**
see **nut**
senses
see **animal**
see **brain**
see **taste**
shark
Volume 3 30–31
Volume 7 **44–45**
sheep
see **farming**
see **hair**
ship
Volume 1 53
Volume 3 38
Volume 7 **46–47**
Volume 8 18–19
shop
Volume 7 **48**
silver
see **gem**
see **metal**
skeleton
Volume 4 55, 59
Volume 7 **49**
Volume 8 30
skiing
Volume 6 20–21
Volume 7 **50**
Volume 8 40–41
skin
Volume 4 34, 55
Volume 7 **51**

sleet
    see **weather**
slug
    see **snail**
smell
    see **nose**
    see **taste**
smog
    see **pollution**
snail
    Volume 4 61
    Volume 5 51
    Volume 6 54
    Volume 7 **52–53**
snake
    Volume 2 10
    Volume 7 20–21, **54–55**
snow
    see **avalanche**
    see **glacier**
    see **rain**
    see **weather**
soccer
    Volume 3 47
    Volume 7 **56**
soil
    see **minerals**
    see **pollution**
    see **rocks**
solar energy
    see **conservation**
    see **fuel**
    see **Sun**
solar system
    see **planet**
    see **Sun**
sound
    Volume 3 4–5
    Volume 7 **57**
South America
    see **continent**

skeleton

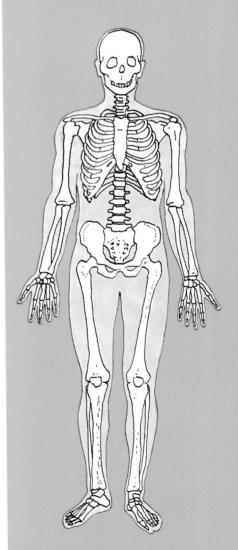

seahorse

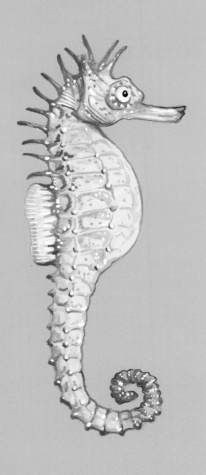

South Pole
> *see* **Antarctica**
> *see* **Earth**
> *see* **latitude and longitude**

Southern Hemisphere
> *see* **equator**
> *see* **season**

spacecraft
> Volume 1 24–25
> Volume 5 58–59
> Volume 7 **58**, 59
> Volume 8 18

space shuttle
> Volume 7 58, **59**

spider
> Volume 4   61.
> Volume 7 **60–61**

sport
> *see* **archery**
> *see* **athletics**
> *see* **baseball**
> *see* **basketball**
> *see* **bicycle**
> *see* **cricket**
> *see* **football**
> *see* **glacier**
> *see* **hang-gliding**
> *see* **hockey**
> *see* **horse-riding**
> *see* **ice skating**
> *see* **netball**
> *see* **Olympic Games**
> *see* **river**
> *see* **rugby**
> *see* **sailing**
> *see* **skiing**
> *see* **soccer**
> *see* **tennis**
> *see* **watersports**

spring
> *see* **season**

squid
> *see* **molluscs**
> *see* **octopus**

stalactite
  see **cave**
stalagmite
  see **cave**
stamp
  see **hobby**
  see **postal service**
star
  Volume 1 26–27
  Volume 4 4
  Volume 7 **62**
  Volume 8 8–9, 28
starfish
  see **echinoderm**
  see **invertebrate**
  see **oyster**
steam engine
  see **train**
steel
  see **iron and steel**
stegosaurus
  see **dinosaur**
stoat
  see **weasel**
stomach
  see **digestion**
  see **human body**
submarine
  Volume 7 **63**
sugarcane
  see **grass**
summer
  see **season**
Sun
  Volume 1 26–27, 30
  Volume 2 4–5, 32–33, 45
  Volume 3 6–7, 12, 13, 46
  Volume 4 30, 38
  Volume 5 22, 28, 59
  Volume 6 44–45, 47
  Volume 7 10, 12–13, 42–43, 62, **64**
  Volume 8 13, 28, 36, 44, 52, 58

Ss

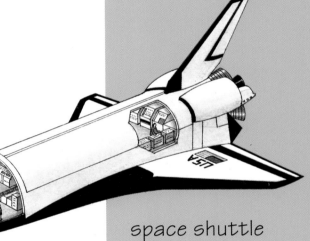

space shuttle

Ss

turtle

swimming
  see **Olympic Games**
  see **water sports**

tacking
  see **sailing**
tadpole
  see **amphibian**
  see **frog**
  see **life cycle**
tapir
  see **rhinoceros**
taste
  Volume 4 55
  Volume 6 11
  Volume 8 **4**
teddy bear
  see **toy**
teeth
  Volume 4 55
  Volume 8 **5**
telephone
  Volume 4 60
  Volume 7 35
  Volume 8 **6–7**
telescope
  Volume 1 26–27
  Volume 8 **8–9**
television
  Volume 7 55
  Volume 8 **10–11**
tennis
  Volume 8 **12**
tent
  see **camping**
  see **house**
terrapin
  see **pet**
  see **turtles and tortoises**
thermometer
  see **heat**
thunder and lightning
  see **weather**

tides
Volume 6 14–15
Volume 7 40–41
Volume 8 **13**

toad
see **amphibians**
see **frog**

toadstool
see **fungi**

tongue
see **taste**

torch
Volume 3 16–17
Volume 5 28–29
Volume 8 **14**

toy
Volume 2 58
Volume 5 12
Volume 8 **15**

traffic
see **motor car**
see **police**

train
Volume 3 57
Volume 8 **16–17**, 18–19

transport
Volume 1 4–5, 8–9, 46–47, 53, 60–61
Volume 2 13
Volume 4 40, 54
Volume 5 60–61, 62
Volume 7 24–25, 26, 46–47, 63
Volume 8 16–17, **18–19,** 22–23, 50–51, 60

tree
Volume 3 48–49
Volume 5 22–23
Volume 6 32–33, 46–47
Volume 7 14–15
Volume 8 **20–21**

triceratops
see **dinosaur**

tree

Uu

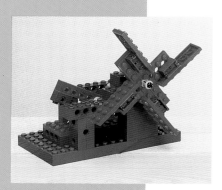

toy

troposphere
    see **atmosphere**
    see **wind**
truck
    Volume 7 26
    Volume 8 18–19, **22–23**
tuatara
    see **reptiles**
turtles and tortoises
    Volume 7 20–21
    Volume 8 **24–25**
typhoon
    see **cyclone**
tyrannosaurus
    see **dinosaur**

underground mining
    see **mining**
underwater mining
    see **mining**
ungulates
    Volume 4 28–29
    Volume 8 **26**
uniform
    see **clothes**
United Nations
    Volume 3 34–35
    Volume 8 **27**
Universe
    Volume 1 26–27
    Volume 3 6–7
    Volume 4 4
    Volume 7 62, 64
    Volume 8 **28**
Uranus
    see **planet**
    see **Sun**

vaccination
    see **doctor**
vegetable
    Volume 3 25
    Volume 6 18, 46–47
    Volume 8 **29**

Vv

Venus
    see **planet**
    see **Sun**
vertebrate
    Volume 1 16
    Volume 8 **30**
veterinarian
    Volume 6 38
    Volume 8 **31**
video
    see **television**
vitamins
    Volume 3 44–45
    Volume 8 **32**
vocal chords
    see **sound**
volcano
    Volume 4 64
    Volume 5 63
    Volume 8 **33**
vulture
    Volume 8 **34–35**

wallaby
    see **kangaroo**
walrus
    see **Arctic**
    see **seal**
warm-blooded animals
    see **bird**
    see **mammal**
water
    Volume 2 43
    Volume 3 32, 39
    Volume 4 56, 63
    Volume 5 19
    Volume 6 14–15, 52–53, 54–55
    Volume 7 10–11, 20–25, 40–41
    Volume 8 **36–37,** 38–39
water beetle
    see **beetle**
    see **pond life**

vulture

Ww

weasel

water cycle
  see **cloud**
  see **rain**
  see **water**
  see **weather**
waterfall
  Volume 7 24–25
  Volume 8 **38–39**
water sports
  Volume 2 13
  Volume 7 34
  Volume 8 **40–41**
weasel
  Volume 8 **42–43**
weather
  Volume 1 19
  Volume 2 26, 31, 42
  Volume 7 10–11, 12–13, 35, 42–43
  Volume 8 **44–47,** 52–53
web
  see **spider**
week
  see **calendar**
  see **days of the week**
whale
  Volume 1 17
  Volume 5 40
  Volume 8 **48–49**
wheat
  see **bread**
  see **farming**
  see **grass**
wheel
  Volume 4 60
  Volume 5 37
  Volume 8 18–19, **50–51**
wildflower
  see **flower**
wind
  Volume 2 42
  Volume 5 12–13
  Volume 8 44–47, **52–53**
winter
  see **season**

Zz

Winter Olympics
  see **Olympic Games**
  see **skiing**
wolf
  Volume 2 56–57
  Volume 6 5
  Volume 8 **54–55**
World Heritage List
  see **heritage**
worm
  Volume 3 9
  Volume 4 61
  Volume 6 54–55
  Volume 8 **56–57**
worm lizard
  see **reptiles**
writing
  see **alphabet**
  see **book**

X-ray
  Volume 2 54
  Volume 8 **58**
xylophone
  Volume 8 **59**

yacht
  Volume 7 34
  Volume 8 **60**
yak
  Volume 8 **61**
year
  see **calendar**
  see **months of the year**

zebra
  Volume 4 28–29
  Volume 8 **62–63**
zoo
  Volume 8 **64**
zoologist
  see **zoo**

zebra

SUBJECT INDEX

- The subject index lists all the entries in the encyclopedia, under different subject headings.
- Under each subject heading, the entries are listed alphabetically, volume by volume.

butterfly

SUBJECT HEADINGS

Animals

Arts and Literature

Astronomy

Business

Geography

History

Human Body

Mathematics

Natural Resources

Our Earth

Plants and Food

Science

Social Education

Sport and Recreation

Technology

Transport

ANIMALS

Volume 1
alligator
amphibians
animal
ant
ape
bat
bear
bee
beetle
bird
butterflies and moths

Volume 2
camel
camouflage
canary
cat
cattle
crab
deer
dog
dolphin
dragonfly
duck

Volume 3
earthworm
echinoderm
eel
egg
elephant
fish
flea
flies
fox
frog

Volume 4
giraffe
goat
goldfish
grasshopper
guinea pig
hair

chimpanzees

ANIMALS

hedgehog
hippopotamus
horse
insect
invertebrate

Volume 5
jaguars and leopards
jellyfish
kangaroo
kiwi
koala
ladybird
life cycle
lion
lizard
mammal
marsupial
molluscs
monkey

Volume 6
nest
octopus
ostrich
owl
oyster
panda
parrots
penguin
pigeon
platypus
quail

Volume 7
rabbit
rat
reptiles
rhinoceros
rodents
seahorse
seal
shark
snail
snake
spider

fox

Volume 8
turtle and tortoises
ungulates
vertebrate
vulture
weasel
whale
wolf
worm
yak
zebra

ARTS AND LITERATURE

Volume 1
ballet
bell
book
Volume 2
cartoon
circus
dancing
drama
Volume 5
library
music
Volume 6
newspaper
orchestra
painting
puppet
Volume 8
xylophone

ASTRONOMY

Volume 1
astronaut
astronomy
Volume 4
galaxy

drama

BUSINESS

GEOGRAPHY

cave

Volume 5
meteor
moon
Volume 6
planet
Volume 7
satellite
spacecraft
space shuttle
star
Sun
Volume 8
Universe

BUSINESS

Volume 1
bank
Volume 5
money
Volume 7
shop

GEOGRAPHY

Volume 1
Antarctica
Arctic
avalanche
Volume 2
cave
continent
dam
desert
Volume 3
earthquake
equator
Volume 4
glacier
iceberg
island

Volume 5
  lake
  latitude and longitude
  mountain
Volume 7
  river
Volume 8
  volcano

HISTORY

Volume 2
  castle
  dinosaur
Volume 3
  fossil
Volume 4
  heritage
Volume 5
  knight
  mammoth

HUMAN BODY

Volume 1
  blood
  brain
Volume 2
  digestion
Volume 3
  ears
  exercise
  eyes
Volume 4
  heart
  human body
Volume 5
  lungs
Volume 6
  nose
Volume 7
  skeleton
  skin

HISTORY

HUMAN BODY

human body

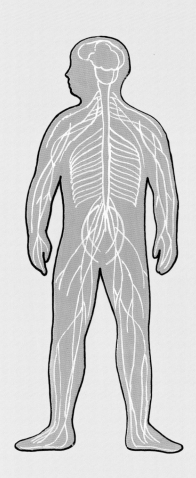

MATHEMATICS

NATURAL
RESOURCES

OUR EARTH

Volume 8
   taste
   teeth

MATHEMATICS

Volume 3
   fraction
Volume 5
   measurement
Volume 6
   number

NATURAL RESOURCES

Volume 1
   aluminium
Volume 2
   coal
   cotton
Volume 3
   electricity
   fuel
Volume 4
   gas
   gem
   glass
   gold
   iron and steel
Volume 5
   metal
   minerals
   mining
Volume 6
   oil
   paper
   quarry
   quartz

OUR EARTH

Volume 1
   air
   atmosphere

mining

Volume 2
cloud
compost
conservation
coral
cyclone
Volume 3
Earth
ecology
endangered species
flood
food chain
Volume 4
irrigation
Volume 6
national park
ocean
pollution
pond life
Volume 7
rain
rainbow
recycling
rocks
seashore life
season
tides
Volume 8
water
waterfall
weather
wind

PLANTS AND FOOD

Volume 1
bread
Volume 3
farming
fern
fishing
flower
food
forest

vegetable market

SCIENCE

SOCIAL
EDUCATION

fruit
fungi
Volume 4
grass
grassland
Volume 5
leaf
Volume 6
nut
plant
Volume 7
rain forest
Volume 8
tree
vegetable
vitamin

SCIENCE

Volume 1
balloon
Volume 2
colour
Volume 3
eclipse
floating
friction
Volume 4
gravity
heat
Volume 5
laser
light
magnet
Volume 7
sound

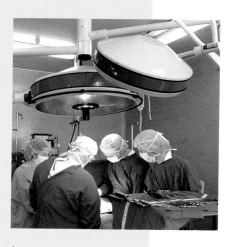

hospital

SOCIAL EDUCATION

Volume 1
airport
alphabet
ambulance
brick

Volume 2
    calendar
    clothes
    days of the week
    doctor
    doll
    dragon
    drug
Volume 3
    festival
    firefighters
    flag
Volume 4
    garden
    hospital
    house
Volume 5
    kite
    lighthouse
    magic
    map
    months of the year
Volume 6
    name
    pet
    pirate
    police
    postal service
Volume 7
    road
    school
Volume 8
    toy
    United Nations
    veterinarian
    zoo

SPORT AND RECREATION

Volume 1
    archery
    athletics

Arctic

baseball
basketball
Volume 2
camping
cricket
Volume 3
football
Volume 4
game
gymnastics
hang gliding
hobby
hockey
horse riding
ice skating
Volume 6
netball
Olympic Games
Volume 7
Rugby
sailing
skiing
soccer
Volume 8
tennis
water sports

TECHNOLOGY

Volume 1
bridge
Volume 2
camera
clock
computer
Volume 4
invention
Volume 5
jet engine
knot
machine
Volume 6
plastic
printing

space shuttle

Volume 7
radar
radio
refrigerator
robot
Volume 8
telephone
telescope
television
torch
wheel
X-ray

TRANSPORT

Volume 1
aeroplane
bicycle
boat
Volume 2
canoe
Volume 4
helicopter
hovercraft
Volume 5
motor car
motorcycle
Volume 7
ship
submarine
Volume 8
train
transport
truck
yacht

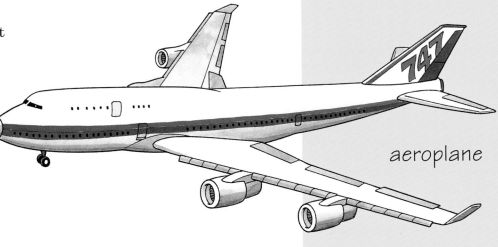

aeroplane